TEN IN A BED

Mary Rees

HOUGHTON MIFFLIN COMPANY
BOSTON
ATLANTA DALLAS GENEVA, ILLINOIS PALO ALTO PRINCETON

Houghton Mifflin Edition, 1996

Printed in the U.S.A.

ISBN: 0-395-75259-0

23456789-B-99 98 97 96 95

There were TEN in the bed

And the little one said,
"Roll over! Roll over!"
So they all rolled over
And one fell out . . .

There were NINE in the bed
And the little one said,
"Roll over! Roll over!"
So they all rolled over
And one fell out . . .

There were EIGHT in the bed
And the little one said,
"Roll over! Roll over!"
So they all rolled over
And one fell out . . .

There were SEVEN in the bed
And the little one said,
"Roll over! Roll over!"
So they all rolled over
And one fell out . . .

There were SIX in the bed
And the little one said,
"Roll over! Roll over!"
So they all rolled over
And one fell out . . .

There were FIVE in the bed
And the little one said,
"Roll over! Roll over!"
So they all rolled over
And one fell out . . .

There were FOUR in the bed
And the little one said,
"Roll over! Roll over!"
So they all rolled over
And one fell out . . .

There were THREE in the bed
And the little one said,
"Roll over! Roll over!"
So they all rolled over
And one fell out . . .

There were TWO in the bed
And the little one said,
"Roll over! Roll over!"
So they all rolled over
And one fell out . . .

There was ONE in the bed
And the little one said,
"I'm not getting up!"
The other NINE said,
"Oh, yes, you are!"

Then there were NONE in the bed
And no one said,
"Roll over! Roll over!"